The Life, Times, and Legacy of Nipsey Hussle

Rapper Extraordinaire

A Biography of an Icon and West Coast Hero

By

JJ Vance

Table of Contents

Before You Go Any Further,.. 5

Download Your Free Gift!.. 5

Nipsey Hussle Introduction and Background............................ 6

    Name & Hussle's Childhood 8

    Busted for Breaking into School 8

Nipsey Hussle's Music Overview 9

Nipsey Hussle's Love for Community and Activism 16

    Charity Work 18

Nipsey Hussle's Music, Mixtapes, Album
and Other Ventures in Detail 19

    Working with Diddy 22

    The Story Behind the $100 Mixtape 23

Nipsey Hussle's Acting 25

Nipsey Hussle's Personal Life 26

    Nipsey Hussle's Love Life 27

    About Tanisha Foster 28

Other Significant Details in the life of Nipsey Hussle 33

    Hussle and YG 37

    Kyle Kuzma 37

    Arrest Record 38

    The Hero "Gang Member" Controversy 40

    Nipsey & Iddris Ssandu 42

    Dean Sean-Jackson & Nipsey Hussle 43

    On Building Vector90 44

    Foreseeing His Funeral 44

    Nipsey Hussle as an Ardent Reader... 45

    Nipsey and Gary Vee 45

    XXL Freshman Class 2010 46

    Nipsey Hussle on Dr Sebi 47

    His Legacy is Part of US History.. 49

Charlamagne & Nipsey Hussle 49

Nipsey Hussle Vs Dj Akademiks 50

Nipsey Hussle & the Game 60

His Last Message 63

Rollin' 60s 64

Nipsey Hussle's Violent History 65

Brawl in West Hollywood 65

BET Awards Incident 65

His Decision to Join the 60s Crip Gang 66

Nipsey Hussle &Kids 66

Hussle as an Entrepreneur 68

The Shooting and Nipsey's Death 70

The Aftermath of Nipsey Hussle's Murder and Various Tributes 72

Nipsey Hussle's Memorial: A Celebration of Life 74

Chaos at His Memorial Service 79

The Legacy of Nipsey Hussle 80

Conclusion 81

Final Surprise Bonus 82

Enjoyed This Book? Then Check Out... 84

Get to know the "Real" 50 Cent - Behind the Curtains 84

Disclaimer and Note to Readers:

This is an unofficial tribute book to Nipsey Hussle from a fan, for a fan to support his legacy.

The information in this book has been provided for educational and entertainment purposes only.

The information contained in this book has been compiled from sources deemed reliable and it is accurate to the best of the Author's knowledge; however, the Author cannot guarantee its accuracy and validity and cannot be held liable for any errors or omissions.

The fact that an individual or organization is referred to in this document as a citation or source of information does not imply that the author or publisher endorses the information that the individual or organization provided. This is an unofficial fan tribute book and has not been approved or endorsed by the Nipsey Hussle or his associates.

Before You Go Any Further,
Download Your Free Gift!

Thanks for checking out **"Nipsey Hussle: A Secret Biography"** – You have made a wise choice in picking up this book!

Because you're about to discover many interesting tidbits of Nipsey Hussle you've never knew before!

But before you go any further, I'd like to offer you a free gift.

My Ultimate Collection of Links to Nipsey Hussle's YouTube Videos!

If you're a Nipsey fan, you'll DROOL over this!

But I'll take it down if too many people claim it as it's my personal treasure. Don't miss out!

Get it before it expires at:
http://jjvance.com/nipseybonus
Or Scan the QR Code:

Nipsey Hussle Introduction and Background

The world of show business is full of inspiring and captivating stories. Several people have made a name for themselves despite starting with nothing. However, show business has its share of tragedy and heartbreak as well. The history of Los Angeles is equally dramatic and full of violence and gang aggression. Nipsey Hussle was at the very intersection of show business drama and Los Angeles life. He was a prime example of a self-made man, rising on his own against the odds. His music was notable for his sharp street observations.

Nipsey Hussle, a well-known rapper and songwriter, is no more after falling victim to a shooting in his neighborhood. Hussle's real name was Ermias Joseph Asghedom. His professional name was often stylized as Nipsey Hu$$le. He was a well-known community activist, businessman and entrepreneur as well. Despite being nominated for a Grammy award, his community work outshines his music. Hussle was born on the 15th of August, 1985 and left this world on the 31st of March, 2019, as a result of a shooting. The shooter, Eric Holder, and the rapper knew each other. According to the investigators, the murder seems to have stemmed from a personal matter between the two men.

Hussle was only 33 when he passed away. His death has shocked Los Angeles, his loved ones, and the rest of the world. A huge number of celebrities have expressed their grief on social media following the death of Hussle. He has left two children, Kross Asghedom and Emani Asghedom.

Hussle was of Eritrean descent on his father's side and African American descent on his mother's side. He was raised by his mother in LA. One of the inspirations behind his community work was his visit to Eritrea, which is a country in East Africa. Hussle grew up in the Crenshaw neighborhood in South Los Angeles. He was part of the local Rollin' 60s, a clique of the Neighborhood Crips gang, at some point in time. He joined it as a teenager. Nipsey bade adieu to his home at the age of 14 and joined the gang for support since he was on his own. However, he did not continue to be a gang member after finding success as a rapper. In fact, he tried to improve the quality of life in his community so that others would not need to join a gang to survive.

Name & Hussle's Childhood

Nipsey was given to him by a childhood friend coined from the Nipsey Russell name while the Hussle was based on his Entrepreneurial spirit.

His hustling days started from childhood, where he polished shoes for $2.50 a pair with a target of $100, which he would use to buy school clothes.

Busted for Breaking into School

According to the guardian, Nipsey Hussle was once caught breaking into a school's computer lab, although he denied the crime.

However, he ended up dropping out of school because of the incident.

Nipsey Hussle's Music Overview

Hussle became known amidst the West Coast hip hop arena in the 2000s. He gained fame for a number of mixtapes, including the *Bullets* series, *The Marathon, Crenshaw*, and several others. He sold copies of the latter for $100 each. Jay-Z purchased 100 copies of this mixtape.

Nipsey Hussle released only one official album, which was released in February 2018 after a long wait and several delays. Prior to the release of the album, he enjoyed phenomenal success in the hip-hop genre. The album was titled *Victory Lap,* and it enjoyed both commercial success and critical accolades. A huge number of people endorsed the album globally. It received a nomination for Best Rap Album at the 61st Annual Grammy Awards in 2019. Hussle had a lot of pride in his work and a strong sense of ownership. When record labels offered him big amounts of money but no significant part in the making of his album, he told them to keep the money but let him have a say in the proceedings. This is why his only album got so late in his release despite being in the works for a long time. He had a huge number of singles, mixtapes, and other work. Nipsey Hussle further played a part in promoting Jay-Z as well.

Hussle's first caught the attention of the corporate music world in 2005, and the first record Label to approach him off the success of the 2005 *Slauson Boy Volume 1* mixtape was a record label known as Epic Records. Hussle later released two other mixtapes (*Bullets Ain't Got No Name Vol. 1 and Vol. 2.*) under the record label.

However, although his albums were greatly appreciated by hip hop fans, all of Nipsey's released music under Epic Record label hardly left an imprint on Billboard charts and got little to no radio play.

Two years later, Nipsey did not only leave Epic Records to go independent, he also did something quite remarkable as an artiste. He shifted his priorities from making money from his music to just making music for his fans that had proved to be loyal. Mixtapes were flowing in steadily – and for free.

And the effect was tremendous.

By 2013, he already had a large number of followers, large enough to try something new and unique:

His next mixtape *Crenshaw,* was dedicated to praising the close, predominantly black community of Crenshaw District in the southern LA area, where the rapper grew up — made waves because of the unique business model he adopted.

Hussle decided to make all digital copies of his album available at no cost at all and sold a thousand physical copies for just $100 each.

And when asked for the reason behind charging such an amount for a CD, he replied, commenting on how he tailors his music to give his ardent listeners top-notch customer satisfaction.

The rapper found support in Jay-Z, who showed the extent of his support for Hussle by immediately snatching up 100 copies, and this went a long way in raising Hussle's profile as a rapper, as well as fueling more response to the album.

After that, the rapper continued to go on tours, while also releasing mixtapes for free, at a consistent rate.

In 2015, Nipsey tweaked the business model used in the release of *Crenshaw* when he released his independent album, *Mailbox Money*.

This time, instead of selling a thousand hard copies at $100 each, he made only 100 hard copies of this new album and made it available for $1,000 each.

Explaining the idea behind the new feat during an interview with Forbes, he pointed out the fact that, an artiste can produce fine works of arts or pure artistic product if they have the knowledge on how to build their own industry to serve them more rather than rely on the capitalistic market to do it for them.

This move did not just put Nipsey and his music on the radar of some of the biggest music executives, but also got him a record deal with Atlantic Records.

Nipsey released Victory Lap, in 2018, which had collaborations with artists like CeeLo Green and Kendrick Lamar.

Now that was a major turning point for the rapper.

Victory Lap earned him a spot on the Billboard album charts, and it did not stop there. A Grammy nomination followed, and both LeBron James and Rihanna joined his fan base.

Nipsey Hussle's legacy did not just come from his music. His legacy was borne out of his strength and ability to channel a past filled with violence into community activism and philanthropy.

There was a deep connection between Nipsey's music and the Rollin' 60s, a group that is tied to the Crips, and mostly based outside Crenshaw. He has always been open about his membership in the gang, which he joined as a teenager. He even spoke proudly about "making it out" untouched, in an interview;

Talking about his section of the Crenshaw District in the Rollin' 60s, he narrated that none of his peers survived the travails of the gang life. Some went to prison while some got into one form of trouble, but it was no simple feat to him to have made it out without any repercussions.

Opening up about what it was like to transition from being involved in gang-violence culture to being an artiste, the rapper said he felt "an ambassador."

According to him, nobody other than Snoop has been able to transition successfully from gang life and also stand as an ambassador simultaneously.

He also added that moving forward, he was in a better and different state of mind and was focusing on giving solutions and inspiration.

Hussle also elaborated on what got him involved in gang and violence.

In an interview with VLAD TV in 2014, he explained how he left home at a young age, out of his mother's house and in with his grandmother.

Hussle built his legacy from the ground up, and philanthropy played a huge role, which he started in 2017 when he partnered with DJ Khaled and bought real estate in the Crenshaw District. This led to the emergence of his clothing store, Marathon.

By the time 2018 rolled around, he had also cofounded a center for the underprivileged neighborhood youths, focused on science and technology.

He admitted that he found his inspiration in the leading giants of Silicon Valley, like Mark Zuckerberg and Elon Musk.

According to him, during an interview with Complex in 2017, one of the major factors Silicon Valley has continually used to justify the lack of diversity in the creative community is the lack of connection from the inner cities to Silicon Valley.

And the reason for this disconnect between Silicon Valley and the inner cities, according to him, was the lack of STEM skills, which he believes cannot be taught theoretically to a 13-year old year but can only be inculcated effectively through practical knowledge and training.

All of the aforementioned, now, raises the question of why?

Why did Hussle, despite his community activism, investment efforts, accolades, and even impressive fan base, not gain an even wider audience before his death.

Perhaps it is because of what GQ's Mark Anthony Green described as the area of the pop-culture industry that White America was yet to exploit?

In other words, Hussle targeted his efforts to and attracted the attention of predominantly black audiences.

In an interview with GQ, he commented on the need to always be appreciated as an artist and how he reads every review but is never a fan of seeking validation through awards or anything controlled by politics.

Nipsey Hussle's Love for Community and Activism

Nipsey Hussle was considered to be a phenomenon and a movement.

Hussle was an icon that extended beyond music. He touched people's lives by giving back to his community and trying to improve the standard of life for people.

Hussle had an easygoing and warm nature. He interacted with everyone in a loving manner. He considered the community to be extremely important and gave back to it to the best of his ability. He tried his best to improve conditions in his beloved neighborhoods and took initiatives to fight violence in LA until his death in March 2019.

Hussle was part of the creators of the art museum known as Destination Crenshaw, which was created to honor the artistic achievements of African-Americans.

Also, he invested in a co-working space which is located in the South Central area of Los Angeles called Vector90, and the place also served as a center for youth to take classes in (STEM) science, technology, and mathematics plus short term leases and office space for Entrepreneurs.

He joined the Crips Gang during a time when the Crenshaw district was rife with violence.

In an interview with Fader, Hussle said he didn't attend school in Crenshaw but West Los Angeles where he had a Korean and a Jewish Buddy who used to copy off his work. While his buddies always got an invitation to take a test in order to be admitted to a "Gifted program," his teachers always looked him over until his mom visited the school and demanded that he be allowed to write the test.

After the test, the teachers ended up apologizing as his "results were off-the-chart."

He regarded himself as the "Tupac of his Generation" in his 2018 album, *Victory Lap.*

Charity Work

Also, in 2010 in light of the aftermath of the 7.0 magnitude earthquake that struck Haiti, Nipsey Hussle was part of the artists featured in the charity single, "We Are the World 25 for Haiti."

Nipsey Hussle's Music, Mixtapes, Album and Other Ventures in Detail

Hussle released his first mixtape titled *Slauson Boy Volume 1* in 2005. He then released the two mixtapes known as *Bullets Ain't Got No Name, Vol. 1 and Vol. 2*. He released his first single "Hussle in the House" in 2009. He released the third volume of *Bullets Ain't Got No Name* in 2009 as well. His notable song appearances included "We Are the World 25 for Haiti" in 2010 and others. Different magazines rated him highly. He became a respected artist, and people took his music seriously.

His debut album, *South Central State of Mind*, was supposed to come out in 2010, but it was postponed until further notice. Hussle had been working with Epic Records until then, but after some issues, the label let him go in late 2010. He then established his own record label, All Money In.

Hussle released his first mixtape with All Money In Records on the 21st of December, 2010. It was called *The Marathon*. He released a sequel, *The Marathon Continues*, on the 1st of November,

2011. Hussle went on to release a joint album called *Raw* with another rapper, Blanco, on the 17th of April, 2012. It includes guest appearances from several notable artists, including YG, Kokane, B-Legit, Yukmouth, Mistah FAB and Freeway. Hussle further released a single "Proud of That" in May 2012, with Rick Ross's guest voice. Hussle featured on the MMG song titled "Fountain of Youth", which is part of the second album of the self-made label Vol. 2. The music video came out on the 1st of October, 2012. In December 2012, Hussle indicated again that he would sign with Maybach Music Group/Warner Bros. Records. However, he also underlined that he would go with the correct choice of label. Rumor had it in 2012 that Hussle would play a role in Rick Ross's Maybach Music Group label (MMG). Nipsey Hussle further appeared in a single by rapper YG. This single was titled "B*tches Is not Sh*t", which showcases the classic Dr. Dre song in a manner. It also features Snoop Dogg and rapper young Money Tyga. The song opened in the American Billboard 100 at number 100 and the Heatseekers Songs chart at number 11.

Hussle emphasized that he would finish the Marathon mix series with *TM3: Victory Lap* in 2013, after the earlier release date of December 2012 being canceled out. He said in an announcement that he had plans to release a mixtape with a West Coast rapper and a YG regular. This mixtape was going to be called *Two of America's Most Wanted* in 2013.

He gave a performance at the "Paid Dues" festival on the 30th of March, 2013, in California. He began releasing different songs from his would-be mixtape *Crenshaw* in 2013. This included the song "Face the World", released by 9th Wonder, and a song by The Futuristic and 1500 or Nothin', titled "Blessings." *Crenshaw* further included songs about growing up in this part of LA.

On the 6th of August, 2013, he announced that he would release *Victory Lap* as an album instead of a mixtape. He was going to share details soon. On the 16th of September, 2013, he declared that his *Crenshaw* mixtape, hosted by DJ Drama, would be released on the 8th of October, 2013. He shared the tracklist for *Crenshaw* on the 24th of September, 2013. It included guest appearances from Dom Kennedy, Rick Ross, James Fauntleroy II, Sade, Skeme, Z-Ro, Slim Thug, and several others. A number of names including The Futuristic, 1500 or Nothin', 9th Wonder, Mike Free, Ralo, Jiggy Hendrix, and others took care of the production. *Crenshaw*, his eighth mixtape, managed to gain a spot on the Top 40 of the Billboard Heatseekers chart. Hussle released the documentary "Crenshaw" while promoting the mixtape the same day. He released 1000 copies of his new mixtape Crenshaw, on the 8th of October, 2013. All these copies were sold for $100 each within 24 hours. He released two compilation albums of great hits on iTunes, *Nip Hussle the Great Vol.*, on the 2nd of October, 2013.

Mailbox Money was released on the 31st of December, 2014. Hussle then had plans to release *Victory Lap* in 2014. He shared with Complex on the 14th of October, 2013, that *Victory Lap*'s first single would be "Rap Niggas" and that it was ready. He later shared the names of those behind the production, including The Futuristic, DJ Mustard, 1500 or Nothin', Ralo, DJ Khalil, and Don Cannon. He released another mixtape called *Famous Lies and Unpopular Truth* in 2016. He released the single "FDT" (Fuck Donald Trump) with YG as a commentary on the 2016 US Presidential Election. This song covered Hussle's positive encounters with Mexican immigrants. FDT gained the number 50 spot on the Hot R&B/Hip Hop Songs chart. In 2017, Hussle went back to his own material with "Still." He released *Slauson Boy, Vol. 2* during the same year, which featured Snoop Dogg, Mozy, Young Dolph, Dave East, G Perico, Kirko Bangz, and Young Thug. He also released a joint project, *No Pressure*, with Bino Rideau before the end of 2017. He released his debut studio album on the 16th of February, 2018. *Victory Lap* featured Cee Lo Green, Kendrick Lamar, The-Dream, YG, Puff Daddy, and others as guest appearances. It opened in the Top 5 of the Billboard 200.

Working with Diddy

Nipsey enlisted the help of Diddy for his debut album, helping it receive critical acclaim. According to Nipsey, during an interview on the Breakfast Club, he revealed that Diddy said the production wasn't loud enough, then went ahead to play him Natural Born Killers by Ice Cube & Dr. Dre and told him to take inspiration from the track.

While on the show, he also commented on the P Diddy's production abilities and how his abilities influenced the Biggie Smalls' record "More Money More Problems".

The Story Behind the $100 Mixtape

Hussle originally planned to release the mixtape for free on popular hip-hop download site, DatPiff.com but changed his mind after reading the book "Contagious" which he said was recommended to him by a mentor. He told Forbes in the second chapter, "a restaurant owner created the first $100 Philly cheesesteak and got ridiculed but got a ton of prominent people interested."

Hussle's outside-the-box thinking and $100 Philly steak gave him the inspiration to kick off the Proud2Pay, which rewarded Asghedom's most committed fans with concerts, priority access to the new material, and one-of-a-kind gifts which could include an old rap notebook or signed photo.

In less than 24 hours, he sold out 1,000 copies of the mixtape at a pop-up store in Los Angeles.

The $100,000 realized from the sale of mixtape went to the servicing of expenses for Asghedom's label, All Money In No Money Out, which Hussle owns a quarter of. (The remaining share of the company is split evenly between Black Sam (Hussle's elder brother), Adam Andhban and Steven Donaldson.)

Out of the 1,000 copies, popular rapper Jay Z bought 100 copies, and here's the story behind that, according to Nipsey.

According to him, it all started in the DM on Twitter when an undisclosed hip-hop journalist reached out and told him Jay Z respects the idea and after which Jay-Z's team reached out and paid for 100 CDs.

Although Nipsey said he didn't get to talk or thank Jay Z for the gesture, but his actions meant he respected what he (Nipsey) did, and Nipsey said the incident humbled him and made all the risk and efforts put in the project worth it.

Nipsey Hussle's Acting

Hussle portrayed a small role in Bone Thugs-n-Harmony's semi-autobiographical film *I Tried* in 2007.

He further acted in the film *Caged Animal/The Wrath of Cain* in 2010. Nipsey Hussle played the role of Ricky – the son of a crime kingpin named Cain, who had come to jail on charges of accessory to murder. The twist in the tale was that the guy he tried to kill was also put into prison at the same time leading Cain to try to help the two get over their differences by making them see their various similarities. Caged Animal is a good film and one great example of Hussle's determination to do whatever he puts his mind to.

He also did a cameo role in the first episode of *Crazy Ex-Girlfriend* in 2015 in the "The Sexy Getting Ready Song".

Nipsey Hussle's Personal Life

Hussle has a daughter named Emani from a previous relationship. He dated actress Lauren London from 2013 until his death in 2019. They have a son named Kross together, who was born on the 31st of August, 2016.

What paved the way for their long-term love story was when London wanted to buy Hussle's mixtapes for her co-stars. After getting the tapes, she began following him on Instagram, and he also followed her in return. They began their relationship after some time.

Nipsey recently praised Lauren for the sacrifice she made for their family. John Singleton picked her for *Snowfall.* She got the role, shot the pilot, and even performed stunts. This was a dream role for her. However, she had to make an extremely tough decision when she started expecting their son. She chose their family.

Lauren also has a 9-year-old son Cameron with Lil Wayne. Nipsey and Lauren tried their best to keep their children away from the spotlight. They usually did not post their children's pictures on social media, with only a few exceptions. When they appeared in GQ in white clothes on a horse, it sparked engagement rumors.

Nipsey Hussle's Love Life

Everyone knows the love story between Nipsey Hussle and Lauren London.

Here is a brief overview.

They started dating in 2013 after they met at the Marathon store, where London came to buy Nipsey's $100 limited edition mixtape for her co-stars on the BET series *The Game*.

After her purchase, she also proceeded to follow Nipsey on Instagram, and Nipsey followed back and made the first move by sliding into her dm.

They both have a son named Kross together, although they both have a child (Cameron Carter & Emias) from past relationships. Lauren was formerly dating rapper, Lil Wayne.

In a joint GQ interview while commenting on the sacrifices his 'wife' had made for the family, he mentioned that Lauren was handpicked by John Singleton for the film *Snowfall*, but Lauren never got to play her role after getting the part and shooting the stunts because she was expecting their baby boy.

They broke up briefly in 2017 but got back together in 2018.

While Nipsey Hussle's relationship with Lauren was a bit known to the public, the love life of Nipsey Hussle before London wasn't something many were aware of.

Before the love affair with Lauren London, Nipsey Hussle had a love affair with Tanisha Foster, who was the mother of Emani.

About Tanisha Foster

The lady who was born Tanisha Foster in the early '80s, goes by the name Tanisha Asghedom on Facebook, although Tanisha and Nipsey were never married.

While on Twitter and Instagram, she goes by the name Chyna Hussle.

She had been with Nipsey as far back as 2002 when they were still teenagers but had a son in 2003, and another son a few years later for different partners.

In 2008, she found out that she was pregnant for Nipsey Hussle, but there were questions over the legitimacy of the child being Nipsey's because, in a documentary about fatherhood, Nipsey said he was excited but was worried because he and Tanisha were not together when she got pregnant.

Either way, they decided to raise the child together. But Nipsey got locked up during that period, and it was while he was behind bars that he picked the name Emani Dior meaning "beautiful faith" in Swahili and said he picked the name because the name started with the letter "E" just like his name.

Emani was born in 2009 with Nipsey and Tanisha co-parenting. Tanisha regarded Nipsey Hussle as the best dad ever, although they weren't always on good terms.

She was always caught repping his clothing brand and wished him on his birthdays and Father's Day, making it obvious that they still had a close relationship with Nipsey's family and friends.

In fact, on Valentine's Day in 2013, they spent Valentine's Day together in Las Vegas, but it was that same year that he met and fell in love with the actress, Lauren London.

They tried to keep the relationship under wraps but posted pictured of each other on social media making it obvious that they were together.

But things got messy in 2014 when Tanisha attempted to tweet Lauren London, but sent the message to the wrong account, but she implied that Nipsey was still in love with her.

This was not the first time she would claim that she and Nipsey were more than just co-parents.

In November 2017, in response to a fan's comment about her and Nipsey reuniting, she replied they never broke up in the first place.

Tanisha has been in the news since the rapper passed away. It all started when it was discovered she wasn't included in the public memorial service but was recognized when his obituary was read.

Also, she is involved in a custody battle with Nipsey's family. Nipsey's sister, Samantha Smith, told the court that she considered Tanisha to be an unfit mother, and in order to ensure continued stability for Emani, she filed for custody of the little girl.

On the 28th of May 2019, the court agreed to place Emani under the care of Samantha, and Tanisha broke down in the court, claiming she hadn't seen her daughter for a long time.

However, she has continued to fight for custody of her child, and in a rant on Instagram, she claimed she talked to Nipsey 30 minutes before he was shot.

Tanisha also mentioned that Nipsey never disrespected her, and she wasn't going to entertain any negativity from anyone on the matter.

That's not all.

The relationship between Tanisha and Nipsey Hussle's family, according to Tanisha, has been a bit rocky as she claims the family hasn't been treating her right since Nipsey's death. According to her, the family kicked her out of the apartment Nipsey rented for her.

Also, she has talked about her relationship with Lauren London, saying there were no ill feelings between the two of them.

Other Significant Details in the life of Nipsey Hussle

Nipsey Hussle's stage name was adapted from Nipsey Russell, a renowned black actor and comedian. Initially, Hussle's friend gave it to him as a nickname.

Despite his lack of a wider audience, Hussle's efforts were not in vain. Instead, they captured the attention of the communities he targeted.

But his efforts didn't go unnoticed by the community he availed himself to. Issa Rae, the HBO's Insecure actress also grew up in South Los Angeles, like Hussle; and in the aftermath of the rapper's death, she told Buzzfeed News about growing up with the rapper, remembering Hussle's support of and influence over local residents, including herself.

Rae, while commenting on the impact of Nipsey Hussle on her and his community, said that his actions and efforts inspired her to want to do the same, but it was really heart-breaking that he met his demise in the same community.

Nipsey Hussle's death has seen his career fly way above the radar than it did while he was alive. However, nothing and nobody can promote Hussle like himself;

Explaining why he was so devoted to renovating an old basketball court in the neighborhood, Hussle said his devotion was the direct impact of the resilient and go-getter mentality most L.A. residents exude wherever they go.

And what is worse than being brutally murdered by a member of the community he was doing so much for— that very same community.

This thought was voiced by Herman Douglas, Hussle's business partner.

Herman Douglas's relationship with Nipsey Hussle formed way before the rapper began to leave his footsteps on the sands of music. The two met in 2003 when young Hussle was selling CDs.

Herman Douglas talked to the LA Times about what happened before the 33-year-old rapper was shot fatally six times in the head and torso, just outside of his clothing store, Marathon Clothing in South Los Angeles.

According to Douglas,

"Nipsey was doing positive things in the community. Trying to save lives and for one of the people that he was trying to save to come back and kill him..."

He also stated that not only would his neighborhood miss him but also people around the world.

Douglas was with Hussle the day he died – within the same hour, in fact.

According to him, the shooting happened while he and Nipsey were talking. In his statement, Douglas said prior to the shooting, the shooter exchanged pleasantries with him and Hussle, told them about being a rapper, bought a burger, then left.

But Douglas narrated that as soon as his back was turned, the shooter came back and shot Nipsey Hussle.

In his opinion, Nipsey Hussle didn't deserve to die in such a way, and the tragic incident for him was a result of jealousy, hate, and envy.

Herman also disclosed that there was indeed no beef between Nipsey Hussle and the person who pulled the trigger on the gun that left him dead contradicting the Los Angeles Police Department's Chief of Police, Chief Michel Moore's report.

The report stated that it was believed that Nipsey and his killer, Eric Holder, had a personal issue with one another, which then led to Hussle's murder.

Hussle's violent past was no secret, as he openly spoke about it. However, over the years, the rapper had distanced himself from the gang he belonged to, switching to community activism, working towards empowering and employing less privileged groups through investments in real estate, establishing science and technology learning centers for teenagers, and other notable efforts in the inner-city of Los Angeles.

Hussle was also reported to have had plans to attend an anti-gang violence meeting on the very day he was murdered, which was supposed to be held not quite long after he and two other men were fatally shot outside his Marathon Clothing store.

Hussle and YG

Hussle and YG were buddies, but this was an unusual alliance as they both belonged to rival gangs in Los Angeles. However, they were able to put aside their differences and formed a rather unique bond, even collaborating on music over the course of their careers.

The friendship, according to YG, started in 2010 at a studio where they met after Hussle had done some time in prison.

Kyle Kuzma

Kyle Kuzma said Hussle inspired a tattoo on him because he was his favorite rapper back in high school. Kyle felt drawn to Nipsey long before the former first arrived on the NBA scene with the Los Angeles Lakers. As Kuz pointed out, he has a tattoo of the TMC flag from Nipsey's sixth mixtape, The Marathon Continues, emblazoned on his left bicep. For Kuz, playing in purple and gold opened the door for him to meet his "idol" whose music inspired him to work his way from Flint to Utah to the league before Nipsey's untimely death.

Also, the Los Angeles Laker's forward said his love for Nipsey Hussle influenced his decision to sign up for PUMA. Puma released apparel from Hussle's Marathon store in September with all the proceeds going to Nip's foundation.

Arrest Record

Nipsey Hussle was once arrested in Burbank for having a bottle of codeine in his car without prescription, and at the time of his arrest, it was discovered that he had an outstanding warrant for driving with a suspended license, but he was later released on a $1000 bail.

Also, according to the New York Times report, Nipsey Hussle was under criminal investigation by the LAPD until the time of his death.

The report says, despite his death, his business partners are still being investigated.

Why?

This is because the authorities believe that the Marathon store was used as a hub of gang-activities, but what is surprising is Nipsey Hussle's effort in his community has largely been geared towards helping people stay away from gang-related activities.

Even the LAPD praised him as a peacemaker, but there is no verified reason why Nipsey and his business associates were being silently investigated before his death.

Another revelation, some years ago, the LAPD went to the landlords to get them to evict Nipsey Hussle and the Marathon store from its location.

But the reason why the city and the LAPD carried out this investigation was never revealed.

However, one of his partners, David gross, revealed some details of the issue.

In an Instagram rant, Gross alleged that the Los Angeles City Attorney was trying to shut down the Marathon and had been investigating Nipsey while he was alive and alongside his team for almost a decade. In the post, he attached a photo of a letter which was allegedly sent by the Deputy City Attorney and also said the Los Angeles City Attorney hated the fact that Nipsey Hussle and his team were able to buy and develop the Slauson Plaza.

He also said that the LAPD and the city's government purposely leaked a controversial letter that threatened to shut down the Marathon store due to "alleged drug and criminal activities", which happened there, and this, according to him, caused problems for the business and affected some potential business deals.

The Hero "Gang Member" Controversy

Despite all of his great contributions, it would surprise you that he was still considered as a 'gang member'.

And here's why.

On the day of the incident of the shooting that led to the demise of the Crenshaw rapper, he was having a conversation with

Kerry Lathan, a man who had just been released and on parole after 25 years in jail for murder.

Lathan had come to collect a shirt at the Marathon store, but the shirt wasn't ready, and Hussle, who was present at the time, told him the shirt was going to be ready next week.

It was during this conversation that shots were fired, which led to the demise of Nipsey Hussle, with a bullet ending up lodged at the base of the spine of Kerry Lathan, that, according to specialists, if removed could leave him paralyzed.

But the real story is the fact while Lathan was recovering, he was re-arrested for engaging with a former gang member (Hussle), a violation of his parole condition.

Lathan was held in custody for 10 days, but his re-arrest didn't go unnoticed as the issue sparked outrage in the black community.

According to a report by the New York Times, even the parole officers couldn't comprehend the connection between Nipsey

Hussle the local hero and the Nipsey Hussle the gang member which the law enforcement painted him as.

Nipsey & Iddris Ssandu

Idris Ssandu is a Ghanaian-American, who at the age of 15, built a mobile software that made it possible for his classmates to find their classroom, which earned him a commendation award from President Barack Obama.

But how is Nipsey Hussle related to this tech genius?

Idris Ssandu who was born in Ghana and raised Los Angeles, California, built the world's first smart retail store popularly known as "The Marathon Store", which is owned by Nipsey Hussle.

Ssandu has worked and developed the algorithms of big tech companies like Uber, and Snapchat & Instagram considers himself a "protégé" of Hussle.

And in an Instagram post about Nipsey Hussle's death, he claimed the reason why he got the critical acclaim he got was because of Nipsey.

He commented on his relationship with the Late Rapper in an Instagram post.

In his post, he clearly stated that the reason why his name became popular within hip-hop circles and the black community was as a result of Nipsey's support and as a protégé of the late rapper, he was ready and willing to continue his life's work.

He also made reference to Nipsey's album, *Victory Lap*, which he believed was a message to him to continue the work he started.

Dean Sean-Jackson & Nipsey Hussle

Sean-Jackson is an NFL player who has been a close friend of the late Nipsey Hussle since childhood and wore customized cleats honoring Nipsey Hussle throughout the 2019 season.

On Building Vector90

While speaking on Vector90, David Gross said Nipsey Hussle used to come in every Wednesday of every week to discuss strategy on plans he had about the place.

According to him, Nipsey was very meticulous about his plans about the establishment.

Foreseeing His Funeral

Before his death in March 2018, Ermias Asghedom seemed to have a vision of his funeral as he describes the details of how he wanted to be remembered when he was gone in his 2016 song "Ocean Views".

In the track, he mentioned being buried amidst funfair with the color blue, which is the color of the Rolling 60s Crip gang and a Stevie Wonder tune playing as well.

Nipsey Hussle as an Ardent Reader

During an Interview on People's Party with Talib Kwali, The Game mentioned that "Nipsey's music could be felt from his interviews. He said, "If you wanna hear a classic Nipsey Album compile twelve interviews," attesting to the intellectual prowess of the late rapper.

The Game said he (Nipsey) tried to get him to read by informing about books he read or e-books, and that brings us to his relationship with motivational speaker and Entrepreneur Gary Vee.

Nipsey and Gary Vee

Gary Vaynerchuk is one of the most popular motivational and performance speakers in the world, but many might not know that he was one of the big fans of Nipsey Hussle as Nipsey was of him.

In a documentary, Gary Vee narrated how he met the late Nipsey Hussle while he was recording the Victory Lap album.

According to him, Gary Vee thinks Nipsey was very thoughtful about the way he produced his songs and he painted such a clear picture of his truth.

Also, he called him a psychologist and a thinker.

Nipsey Hussle believed that he and Gary Vee have a unique perspective on entrepreneurship and a deep sense of information/knowledge.

For Nipsey Hussle, Gary Vaynerchuk represented a school of thought that went against the cliché way of doing things.

XXL Freshman Class 2010

In 2010, as part of its yearly celebration of upcoming talents to watch out for in the rap industry, XXL Magazine featured Nipsey Hussle alongside J Cole, Wiz Khalifa on its cover for the popular Freshman Class of 2010.

He was named "most determined" of his class and the LA Weekly called him the "Next Big LA Emcee".

Also, Nipsey Hussle provided jobs for convicted felons at his Marathon Clothing store, taking into consideration how hard it was to get a job with a conviction record.

Nipsey Hussle on Dr Sebi

In 2018, during a Breakfast Club interview, Nipsey announced that he would be directing a documentary film on famous herbalist Dr. Sebi.

In the Interview, Nipsey mentioned that although he hadn't met Dr. Sebi before his death, he was a fan of his products, and he believes the holistic doctor was killed.

According to him, the reason why Dr. Sebi was killed was because he threatened the revenue of big pharmaceutical firms, and he stated in the interview that he was doing a documentary on the 1985 trial of Dr. Sebi.

Based on Nipsey's version of Dr. Sebi's trial, he published a newspaper claiming he could cure AIDS and was taken to court by the State of New York, but he won by showing proof to the jury that he could, in fact, cure the disease.

But the Wikipedia version is different.

Apparently, Dr. Sebi went to trial against the state of New York in 1987 for publishing a newspaper that he cured AIDS and was acquitted according to Wikipedia after undercover operations failed to provide enough evidence that he had made a medical diagnosis of the purported conditions.

However, when asked the reason for wanting to do a documentary on the late Dr. Sebi, he said the story of the trial where Doctor Sebi convinced the jury on the methods he used to cure AIDS was a powerful narrative that needed to be told.

Clearly unfinished, Nick Cannon has hinted at the fact that he would be completing the film through a series of Instagram posts.

However, the family of Dr. Sebi ,during an interview on *BET's Black Coffee*, dismissed the popularly 'conspiracy theory" that Nipsey was assassinated based on his work on Dr. Sebi's documentary.

His Legacy is Part of US History

Nipsey Hussle's contributions to his community in South Los Angeles were archived by the United States Congress on the 10th of April, and it was submitted by Democratic Rep, Karen Bass.

The legacy contained details of Nipsey Hussle's contribution and connection to his community.

In her submission, the congresswoman explained how Nipsey influenced the black community by creating awareness around the power that is attached to being a black person.

Charlamagne & Nipsey Hussle

In 2015, popular host of the breakfast club, Charlamagne, had a brief disagreement with Nipsey Hussle when the popular OAP made a comment about Lauren London, who at the time happened to be Nipsey Hussle's girl.

The tweet "Lauren London left her waist trainer at home" remarked on Lauren's weight when she appeared at the 2015 Bet Awards.

And Nipsey replied with a tweet tagging Charlamagne, "Since we are sharing our sense of humor on social media today" with a link to a YouTube video of Charlemagne being jumped by some guys in front of a radio station.

However, Charlamagne replied with a tweet apologizing. The tweet read "I'm pussy. That guy is actually dead now. He got shot from what I heard. Didn't know that was your girl tho. My fault."

Nipsey Hussle Vs Dj Akademiks

Nipsey Hussle was once invited as a guest on *Complex's Everyday Struggle* with Dj Akademiks, but the episode was never released. Apparently, Nipsey walked out in the middle of the show because he wasn't comfortable with some of the issues raised.

And this was no rumor as Nipsey confirmed the incident actually happened on WGCI Chicago and made comments about one of the show's hosts, Dj Akademiks.

Hussle called Akademiks a weirdo and a clown.

He believed Akademiks was hiding behind the safety of his show to stir up controversial issues and would be attacked in the streets for comments he made on his show.

According to him, DJ Akademiks' attempt to stir up controversial issues was an act of instigation and could get him into a lot of trouble which could put him out of the spotlight.

Also, he mentioned that with the path Akadmiks chose, he was definitely going to cause his own downfall.

And in response to Nipsey's comment, DJ Akademiks released a video narrating what happened.

I'm gonna give you the full truth y'all know how I don't lie but basically Nipsey Hussle was on a... I believe a radio show a talk show in Chicago I don't know who the host is but it looks like he has some issue with me whatever but when my name came up, Nipsey had less than kind words to say about me okay basically he said that y'all supposed to be an everyday struggle I walked out he's on some bozo shit this sat in the third instigating blah blah blah okay now let me give you out what actually went down because he just gave the abridged version, let me give you the full version yeah I know I love to talk so take a seat get some popcorn pause the video and listen to the story now if you guys don't know I do a show called everyday struggle.

It's a debate show, we talk about hip-hop topics topics about rappers newsworthy topics okay are some of the topics gossipy? yeah by the way it's a full-on show that's produced by multiple people okay we have a person that their sole job is to come up with topics and they got a rundown of shit we're gonna talk about you know how they come up with these things they come up with them by looking at the new cycle from the day before okay so if someone drops a big song like say Drake drops a big song you're gonna talk about it the next day.

If there's a big event that happened unfortunately if somebody gets jumped if somebody got shot if something noteworthy happened to a rapper or something happen to hip-hop we're gonna talk about it.

Now Nipsey also was on his press run for victory lap and not one that came out like two weeks ago did pretty good in sales if you don't know he's signed to Atlantic now he booked and he confirmed to come up to everyday struggle now understand rappers be on a promotional run shit and clearly he wanted to come up to speak about his album however, we're not an interview show I mean if you guys never watch every day's struggle it's a debate show it's a topic focused show we don't care if you're President Obama we don't care who you really are we're gonna talk about what's hot for the day but of course we're gonna address what's going on with you so if you have an album will promo it or talk about it the beginning or the end but we gotta talk about topics now this is what happens.

So the morning Nipsey Hussle is coming by the way I don't believe I've ever said anything negative about Nipsey that he might feel this way also to keep it real the only critique I've ever had of him and it was like a joint critique of him and yg they had made a comment to say if people don't get that fuck donald trump songs number one they're not doing their job and I'm like come on come on you can't just make a song saying fuck Donald Trump and hope everybody support it cuz I don't like Donald Trump make a really hot song and then they'll go no more. Only critique ever! Morning of everyday struggle, I'm basically there Nipsey and his whole crew there in the green room or whatever the case is we have our separate room that we're in basically our producer goes to Nipsey that he's not blindsided and says hey check out the things we're gonna be talking about.

Apparently either Nipsey's rep PR person whatever didn't really convey to him what type of show it is he looks at the rundown and by the way this is a day after Takashi got into a fight at La very big topic at least for that day in hip-hop.

Takashi was like he gotta fight with some other guy every he was talking about it next to an everyday struggle you have to talk about it right? now it's the first thing that's on our rundown on our topic rundown now I guess our producer shows him the thing and says yo these are the topics now in addition to takashi getting a fight we're also talking about Birdman and his documentary we were talking about some other things I think Diddy we're talking about a wide variety of topics but the rundown started with probably the biggest news of that day.

Nipsey says to our producer I ain't about Takashi! I don't talk a lot of period okay specifically he says I don't want all the headlines from this interview to be Nipsey says this about Takashi okay clearly just try to say I know anything I say is gonna be a bunch of headlines talking about what I just said about him okay and again this is where we were at.

So our producer comes up says ain't online Nipsey don't wanna talk about nobody okay so we look around and we're like this is a debate show again we're not doing interviews, we have to debate now I was even before I said we could cut the Takashi topic because maybe he see stuff in line online and he probably thinks I'm trying to bait him into a question or get him to talk about Takashi which I wasn't I really only wanted to ask him one question it wasn't even about Takashi I was gonna divert that whole conversation to listen you're from the West Coast use somebody you about that life what's up with this checking-in thing and who got a check-in?

Please let me know because this is important for people who are seeing everything unfold from the weekend of NBA all-star weekend and they're confused what this checking-in means so that's the question I was really gonna ask him so we didn't ask too much gotcha now is it what is Takashi thinking or not I don't know clearly at first he said he was down to not talk he don't talk about any other men it's a debate show bro you can't come to a debate show and again I won't even fully blame him because clearly he wasn't up on speed with everything we did on the show or his reps didn't tell him that hey you're gonna go there and you guys gonna do topics so he didn't want to do any topics didn't want to talk about Takashi okay at first I told my I said yeah we could kill the Takashi topic we were not talk about it okay what about the other topics because I was excited to talk about Nipsey. I was excited to see him and talk to him now anyway clearly he was not into talking about anything any topics that we had on the lineup and our producers told him it's not gonna work and I believe he politely left okay he didn't leave saying fuck you whatever and clearly he seemed to be fine so I thought I would never have to speak on that because again it seemed amicable maybe was just a miscommunication his reps didn't tell him that yo they do like topics every day you're gonna have to give your opinion on other artists other artists music and just other shit happen in the culture.e okay that's just the type of show this I figured our talking up as yo he didn't get that memo from his reps so of course he came in not wanting to talk about people cuz he's just trying to promote his album and because of that he said you know what fucking let's not even do the show he left we did the show without him that day and everything was fine so this conversation he's having with this gentlemen is very surprising to me and and by the way maybe this is just how he thinks in general but regardless it's just really no fucking sweat off my back okay again I don't know what his deal is if it was the everyday struggle thing maybe he saw the topics and thought I was responsible for that no I'm not okay I mean could I tell him to change the topic yeah but a lot of times our producer knows what he's doing like he puts a topic that are relevant okay again I don't know what Nipsey Hussle 'he's whole thing is i've said nothing but positive things about his album but such is life you can't expect everybody to like you and also i will say this about other people in the media yeah act like you I don't do almost everything that I do it almost the same motherfucking way in terms of reposting content in, terms of talking about stuff in terms of asking people's opinions and doing hypotheticals but of course again it feels like it's one of those things where the more notoriety you get more people are gonna point fingers at you for either "ruining the culture" or quote any other situation that arises again it comes with the position that I happen to be in now to nipsey I was thoroughly confused by this got a lot of love for your music it's okay a lot of love for me I wish you the best and I mean his album was still good yeah I could go check it out but I just want to explain that because I know anything negative about me go super viral and when there's no explanation people say this is fact.

But the beef between them didn't end there as Nipsey Hussle had a few thoughts on Dj Akademiks on some comments he made about the rapper, 21 Savage.

Nipsey gave his opinion during his appearance on the New Hip Hop News podcast.

So, apparently the rapper 21 Savage declared that he was going to stop buying jewelry and spend more money on investing, but DJ Akademiks criticized 21 Savage's decision to do this and said it wasn't what he expected from a hardcore rapper such as 21 Savage.

According to Akademiks, he didn't want to hear lyrics about investing but rather lyrics about killing and violence-related content from the rapper.

And this opinion didn't sit well with many people, and Nipsey Hussle was one of them.

In Nipsey's opinion, Dj Akademiks was not the right person to give such advice and believed such utterances should be punishable because it was simply unacceptable.

Dj Akademiks attempted to defend himself by alleging that Nipsey was dissing him to promote his new album.

But Nipsy replied to him almost immediately and tweeted a reminder about how he had been treating people who crossed his path long before he started his rap career.

However, the interesting thing about this beef is that DJ Akademiks, while on the Everyday Struggle show, claimed that he squashed the beef with Nipsey before he died.

According to him during an episode of *Everyday Struggle*:

I and Nipsey and we spoke like men for about three hours. It was probably one of the most productive conversations I've had because we were trying to get to a place and of understanding of each other rather than like just argue online or stuff going elsewhere

What I realized and I took away from that conversation about him is that Nipsey is and was a man of the community. He was community first, you know like his whole points in the stuff he was saying to me is that "you're an act you have a really big platform you know I'm a rapper I have a platform as well and while other people might use their platforms differently, I know that there are people who come from areas and places like me they need to see certain things that they could make decisions that better themselves".

So you know the conversations we had it was really trying to get to a point of not only bettering ourselves as men but better and people around him.

And that's how I look at Nipsey as probably the example and one of the guys who were leading the charge in showing rappers you're supposed to really establish businesses, give back and this was the appropriate way.

I think it's so sad because what he was doing was further in the whole culture he was further than a mindset was furthering people just in terms of black business and to see this happen you know it's like we were talking like a couple steps forward and now it seems ruined.

Nipsey Hussle & the Game

This might come as a surprise to many but at one point in time, there seemed to be beef between rapper The Game and Nipsey Hussle.

On the 25th of June 2018, while he was at the BET, The Game posted a video of three guys trying to burglarize his home and he captioned it.

So this past weekend while I was at the BET Awards 3 CRABS ass niggas tried to break into my Muthafuckin home. Guess what? I found out who those Crips/Crabs were that ho a** bit** a** Nigga Nipsey had sent his rolling Crab Niggas at my house. I recognize one in the hoodie, I guess Nipsey was mad one of my piru blood was finna beat his ass and he didn't punch no he slapped the Nigga hahaha like dude wtf!

But anyways those 3 niggas lucky I was not at the house because if I was at my house would kill all three of them on plain site.

But in another post on the incident, no mention of Nipsey was made. Rather in the new post, he just mentioned how the criminals tried to burglarize his home but were unable to find a way in due to the presence of the rottweilers in his house.

He also mentioned that the plate number of the burglars was visible as the CCTV camera of the neighbors captured it and dared the burglars to come back if they could and promised he wasn't going to leave any of them alive.

This puts a question mark on the beef between the two, but one thing was evident before the passing of Nipsey was that whatever beef happened was quashed fast as The Game publicly supported Nipsey Hussle despite belonging to rival gangs.

While doing one of his "one-post-per-day" commemoration of Nipsey on his Instagram page, he revealed that his friendship cost him some vital gang connections.

He mentioned that he had a couple of fights with gang members when he took Nipsey on tour and said some of his people were still not cool with the particular incident till the present day but he had to explain to them that the movement of solidarity which he started by going on tour with Nipsey was bigger than their respective gang differences and a cooperative state of mind with the other gangs could only bear fruitful results.

What most might not know is how the two LA rappers from bitter rival gangs met and built a brotherly union.

During an appearance on Talib Kwali's *People's Party*, the Game narrated how he met Nipsey Hussle.

He said he was driving through the Crenshaw neighborhood when he was crossed by a car full of Crips while waiting at a traffic light and as a blood gang member, his first instinct was danger, but it happened to be Nipsey and a couple of friends in the car.

Then, he introduced HIMSELF AND HIS GANG as the Slauson boys and gave the Game his CD.

The Game also commented on the confidence Nipsey Hussle and his gang had, which he remarked was unlike most of his fellow upcoming artists at the time.

Another commentary was the resemblance Nipsey Hussle had with Snoop Dogg in appearance and style of rap.

So, later that same day, they recorded a song together "They Roll" and 2 other songs.

His Last Message

The day he was murdered, Nipsey tweeted that strange message. Prior to his shooting on that day, the Crenshaw rapper tweeted something about how having strong enemies was a form of "blessing"; a sign which for most people meant something was wrong.

Days leading up to his death, Nipsey Hussle was said to be shooting a music video in Inglewood, California, with DJ Khalid and John Legend according to a tweet posted by John Legend.

Over concerns for his safety, 10 armed policemen were reportedly hired to stand guard, and this was because Nipsey Hussle and the members of the production crew were scared someone would sneak on set to kill him.

Rollin' 60s

Nipsey Hussle wasn't ashamed of his gang ties and infused his affiliation in his music but claimed he wasn't promoting the lifestyle; he was just 'speaking on it'.

Nipsey Hussle's Violent History

With the image of a community hero, Nipsey Hussle was not without his shortcomings and here are a few that you might not know about the late rapper.

Brawl in West Hollywood

The whole incident happened on the evening of Nipsey Hussle's girlfriend, Lauren London's birthday. According to TMZ, the fight broke out in a club's parking lot in West Hollywood when a man mistook him for someone who had started a fight earlier that evening, and this led to some fist throwing before the intervention of club's security and the police.

BET Awards Incident

Most might not know but Nipsey Hussle was officially named a suspect in popular "BET Awards Slap Incident" where Nipsey Hussle slapped a security personnel after he knocked down a cone from the hands of his bodyguard when they tried to park in a restricted area.

His Decision to Join the 60s Crip Gang

According to him in an interview with Vladtv, at the young age of 14, Nipsey Hussle left his mom's house to live with his grandma but was basically independent and hustled to get money to promote his music.

As a result of his hustle, he moved around a lot in a community that was known for its gang-related lifestyle and violence, and it was during this period that he got influenced to join the 60s Crip gang.

Nipsey Hussle &Kids

Apparently, after his death, some Nipsey Hussle fans tried to raise money for his family and notable among them was Reggie Bush who created a go-fund-me account and personally put $10,000 in the account.

However, the account was taken down after the family put out a statement saying they weren't struggling financially and didn't ask anybody to create anything.

And also, his partner (Lauren London) was never asked for permission before the account was created.

According to a report by Page Six, Hussle had quite a financial portfolio, owned all of his recording masters, had 14 different businesses and created multiple trust funds for his children presumably from the money he made from these businesses.

Apart from his kids, he was also working on a foundation for Crenshaw kids before he passed. He wanted to reconstruct school playgrounds, build parks in the area, and kick start STEM programs for Crenshaw students.

Hussle as an Entrepreneur

Hussle inaugurated the Marathon Clothing store on the 17th of June, 2017, in which he was a partner. His Marathon store enabled him to sell his music, clothing and relevant merchandise without any middle person. He made the most of his connections. He further allowed the community to enjoy a distinctively special connection in his life. He inspired several entrepreneurs to go their own way and experiment. He made it easy for people to follow his footsteps. He was a trailblazer in every sense of the word.

The spearhead of The Marathon Agency, Steve Carles, shared with Billboard in October 2016 that Hussle had invested more than six figures in the firm. He also indicated that Hussle was a kind of silent partner. Nipsey carved his own music path by going the independent way. He did things his own way but did them smartly. While a majority of mixtapes are free, he made $100,000 within 24 hours with Crenshaw. Nipsey Hussle brought something unique to rap.

In 2017, Hussle delved into the business of real estate in partnership with DJ Khalid and bought some real estate in Crenshaw including the area that housed Nipsey's clothing store, The Marathon.

The clothing store was created as an avenue to promote commerce in the not-so affluent area of Crenshaw and also as an experiment that blends smart technology with brick-and-mortar retail: Consumers can use their smartphones in the store to order directly from the brand, and Hussle described the environment as having a Starbucks-like vibe.

On the 17th of June 2017, The Marathon Clothing opened for business in Los Angeles, California. The store was created in collaboration with Hussle's brother, Samiel Asghedom, alongside partners like the consulting firm of Steve Carless and Karen Civil.

The Shooting and Nipsey's Death

Hussle was targeted in the Hyde Park area of Los Angeles. He was shot once in the head and five times in the torso. Two other people were also shot but they survived the shooting. According to the investigators, Hussle and the shooter knew each other, and the shooting must have stemmed from a personal matter.

He was shot in broad daylight, in front of a surveillance camera. He was immediately taken to the hospital by paramedics and his family and friends joined him shortly. Nipsey Hussle's death occurred approximately 35 minutes after he was shot outside his store, Marathon. His cause of death was gunshot wounds to the head and torso. He died at 3:55 pm on 31st of March.

Eric Holder, the man who shot him, was arrested and charged later. He had argued with Hussle earlier that day. After shooting Hussle, the gunman kicked his body and ran away. The shooter has pled not guilty to the charges. Even though Hussle's shooting was related to a personal clash, it unfolded amidst a spike in gang-related violence in south LA during March.

Hussle recently bought the strip mall in which housed The Marathon. He was trying to revitalize it as part of his overall attempt to breathe life into the neighborhood where he spent his growing years. He did not want others to fall victim to gang life like him earlier. Hussle's store is a representation of everything that he had achieved, and it is tragic that he lost his life in front of it.

He was supposed to meet LAPD Chief Michael Moore and Police Commissioner Steve Soboroff to discuss how to prevent gang violence and improve living and safety conditions for children on the 1st of April.

The Aftermath of Nipsey Hussle's Murder and Various Tributes

Nipsey Hussle's family held a private ceremony before the public memorial. It was announced that Nipsey's memorial will be open to fans. His public memorial's tickets were finished within an hour.

The murder has left a huge number of people extremely shocked and sad. In the aftermath of Nipsey Hussle's murder, tributes and condolences poured in from a huge number of people. Former President Obama also paid his tribute to Nipsey Hussle. Other than musicians and other celebrities, several NBA players also communicated their sorrow. LeBron James expressed on Instagram that the news of Nipsey's death is really bad. Kyle Kuzma gave Nipsey the credit of his success and motivation. The Minister of Information of Eritrea also paid tribute to Nipsey Hussle's memory. The murder also adds to the debate on gun violence and whether we should boost gun-control initiatives or not. Artists like Riahanna, Snoop Dogg and John Legend have also paid tribute to Nipsey Hussle.

Pharrell Williams expressed his sorrow on the death of an artist who inspired millions who will keep his legacy alive.

Hussle's fans gathered at the murder scene and paid a tribute to Hussle's memory with candles, songs and tears. Many channels broadcasted videos showing this. Following Hussle's death, two women were shot at a vigil held for him outside his store. An intersection in South Los Angeles (the Slauson and Crenshaw intersection) will be renamed after him. This intersection is located in the centre of the area where Hussle spent his growing years.

After his death, Kodak Black announced aspirations to date Lauren London and wait for a year for her to mourn Hussle. He has been heavily criticized by many and banned from several platforms. Among those who criticized him were The Game and others.

Hussle's mother shared a video message following his death in which she expressed her strength and asked others to adopt the same approach. Her resolve, despite her grief, has been rare and extremely inspirational.

Nipsey Hussle's Memorial: A Celebration of Life

Hussle's three-hour memorial was held at the Staples Center, which has the capacity to house 21,000 people. Fans wore white and blue. The closed casket service began an hour late. The arrangement consisted of a huge number of purple flowers and gloomy lighting. A small Eritrean flag hung off the upper rim on the right.

In the initial portions of the ceremony, a photo montage of Nipsey from infancy, childhood and adulthood, with his family, London and with other rappers was played, set to Frank Sinatra's "My Way".

The highlights from Nipsey Hussle's memorial included a letter from former U.S. President Barrack Obama, a song by Stevie Wonder, and a speech by Snoop Dogg. The Los Angeles public memorial on the 11th of April, 2019, was attended by family, friends and thousands of fans.

Obama's letter to Nipsey's family was read by Nipsey's friend and business partner, Karen Civil. Obama praised Nipsey's efforts to transform his neighborhood from a gang-centric place into a better one. Obama's letter underlined and praised Nipsey's ability to recognize hope amidst all the gloom, bullets and gangs surrounding the Crenshaw neighborhood. Nipsey was committed to the attempts to create a co-working space and a skills-training center in the neighborhood.

Snoop Dogg mentioned Nipsey's past link with the Crips gang and how he used that to fight gang violence. Snoop Dogg called him a 'peace advocate' because of his diverse efforts to make things better for the community. Stevie Wonder called Hussle's death unnecessary and asked for tougher gun laws. Stevie Wonder played "Rocket Love" (Nipsey's favorite) and his version of Eric Clapton's "Tears in Heaven." In his 2016 song, "Ocean Views", Hussle expressed his wish for a Stevie Wonder song to be played at his funeral. His wish came true when Stevie Wonder played one of his favorites.

Nation of Islam leader, Louis Farrakhan, stated that Hussle was to rap and hip hop what Bob Marley was to reggae. He went on to state that Hussle beat the pull of gravity to leave gang life.

Hussle's mother and girlfriend, Lauren London, also shared their dearest stories about him during the service. Lauren London shared a text message she sent Nipsey in January, in which she had called him "my turn up and my church." Lauren London read this message she had sent him as she observed him sleep recently. In the message, she had told him that she felt true happiness in her heart when she was around him. She felt safe and shielded. She was completely herself with him. She had also told him that he had turned her into more of a woman and given her a chance to really love a man. She praised his quest for knowledge. She would joke about his habit of listening to audiobooks before he fell asleep. Lauren called Nipsey's soul 'majestic'. She called him the strongest man she had ever known, a soft father, a 'patient leader' and a 'divine light.' She also shared how she had learned a lot from Nipsey, who was her protector and provider. She expressed sorrow that their son would not remember his father's love on his own. She showed a fresh tattoo of Hussle on her forearm after the service. She expressed that 'real love never dies' in an Instagram post and promised that when people see her from now on, they will always see Hussle. She carried her two-year-old son with Hussle, who was in a blue suit, on stage.

Hussle's mother, Angelique Smith, shared her peace with the crowd. She highlighted that Hussle is a legacy. She shared with the crowd that both she and Nipsey's grandmother had felt death coming toward their family prior to the shooting. She referred to her late son as a 'superhero', who did not shy away from leading. She still feels complete. She also told a story about the courage of her son when he was just a boy. Hussle's little sister talked about living in a world which does not have him anymore. His father reminisced about his fighting spirit since the moment he was born.

Snoop Dogg also noted how Nipsey was entirely unique when he approached him with his mixtape. Unlike other rappers who promise to make the other party a million dollars, Nipsey just asked Snoop Dogg to listen to his music. Dogg noted how Nipsey Hussle had vision. Kendrick Lamar also talked about the huge loss.

London's son with Lil Wayne , Cameron Carter, also paid tribute to Hussle. He shared that some days after Nipsey's death, he had a dream about Nipsey. In the dream, Nipsey told Cameron that heaven was like paradise. Cameron also shared with the audience that Nipsey would watch him through the window sometimes and utter the word "respect." When Cameron asked the crowd to say "respect" together, it echoed all over the auditorium.

His friends and family promised to keep his work going. London promised that they would continue to support young minds at his STEM education centers and coworking spaces. She exclaimed, "The marathon continues." She stated that the final act of love is grief. Hussle's brother, Samiel Asghedom, discussed how Hussle would bring different components together to create his first computer. Emotion gripped Samiel when he talked about Ermias aka Nipsey leaving his 'heart and soul' on the intersection of Slauson Avenue and Crenshaw.

The service was so grand and emotionally moving that everyone who witnessed it felt sorry for the loss of Nipsey Hussle.

This was the first celebrity funeral at the Staples Center since Michael Jackson's in 2009. It finished with a video montage in tune to Nipsey's own song, "Dedication."

A 25-mile procession covered the streets of south LA after the memorial. A hearse containing Nipsey's casket was part of the procession. A flag of Nipsey's father's country, Eritrea, was wrapped around Nipsey's casket. This procession drew thousands of people to the streets to have a glance at Nipsey's body. Police monitored the crowd. Four people were shot in the area, but it was not related to the procession carrying Nipsey Hussle's casket. It sheds light on the worsening law and order situation in LA.

Hussle was buried at the Forest Lawn-Hollywood Hills cemetery on Friday afternoon (12th April), which is the final resting place of a huge number of other celebrities including Carrie Fisher, Debbie Reynolds, Bette Davis and others as well. His family was witnessed at his private burial.

Chaos at His Memorial Service

There was a stampede during the April 1st candlelight procession and a memorial erected in honor of the late rapper was destroyed, but volunteers were able to clean up and restore things.

The Legacy of Nipsey Hussle

Nipsey Hussle could have just capitalized on and enjoyed his success, and no one would have questioned him. However, he decided to be much more than that and use his success to improve conditions in ghettos. His grit is evident from the fact that he created a life for himself despite growing up in the violent streets of LA. His birth and death both occurred in LA. He conquered hardship to beat the odds and receive a Grammy nomination. He was an influential community leader.

His entrepreneurial shrewdness is evident from the detail that he was able to rise from a gang-centered childhood to be a celebrated musician and respected philanthropist. His humanitarian attempts were not superficial. He had an in-depth approach toward philanthropy and meant to make things better for people. He lived for people and meaningful connections.

Nipsey Hussle's music and legacy will always stay alive in the hearts of his fans. His community work will continue to provide an improved foundation for generations. He is among the chosen few who live in both worlds after their demise. He is alive in our hearts.

He could not witness how everyone got united during his memorial for a good purpose.

Conclusion

A lot of things might still be unknown about the personality of the Late Nipsey Hussle, but one thing that was evident, on the various aspects of his musical works, businesses, relations and love life, was an influence to reckon with on and off the streets.

Final Surprise Bonus

Final words from the author...

Hope you've enjoyed this biography of Nipsey Hussle.

It was an utmost privilege performing deep research and bringing forth these information to the public for you to enjoy.

I always like to overdeliver, so I'd like to give you one final bonus.

Do me a favor, if you enjoyed this book, please leave a review on Amazon.

It'll help get the word out so more people can find out more about our beloved superstar to support his legacy! (Plus, it'll help me a lot too. Thanks in advance!)

If you do, as a way of way of saying "thank you", I'll send you one of my most cherished collection report– Free:

Nipsey Hussle: The Complete Discography Collection From The Beginning to the Very End

A complete list of all of Nipsey Hussle's work that was ever published (or not published). As a Nipsey Hussle's fan, you'll find this utmost valuable and cannot be missed!

Here's how to claim your free report:

1.   Leave a review

2.   Send a screenshot to: jjvancebooks@gmail.com

Receive your free report –*"Nipsey Hussle: The Complete Discography Collection From The Beginning to the Very End"* – *immediately*!

Enjoyed This Book? Then Check Out...

50 Cent – A Candid Biography of A Self-Made Hustler: The Life And Times Of Curtis "50 Cent" Jackson; Rapper, Singer, Songwriter, Actor, Entrepreneur, Investor by JJ Vance

Get to know the "Real" 50 Cent - Behind the Curtains

Here's Just a Taste What You're About to Hear in This Concise Curtis "50 Cent" Biography:

Things most people might not know about Curtis "50 cent" Jackson

Origin of the name "50 cent"

By 1996, after Curtis was signed by RUN D.M.C, he adopted the name 50 Cent, a name which was inspired by a petty criminal by the name of Kelvin Martin, who used the same name. When asked why he chose the name, he said he chose it because it was a metaphor for change, which implied that he was going to do things his own way that was drastically different from the way others did. In his words, "the name says everything he wanted to say because he had the same 'go-getter' attitude as the original 50 Cent."

The 9 Bullet story

Most people know that 50 Cent was shot nine times, but there are parts that most people don't know about the incident. For instance, during the shooting, 50 Cent said he had a gun while he was being shot at, and while he tried to fire back, he discovered that the gun was not cocked. Also, another thing most people might know is that the doctors who were operating on 50 Cent tried to carry out a tracheotomy, a procedure which involved them opening 50 Cent's wide pipe and which could potentially destroy his chances of ever rapping again.

His grandma, however, refused. She said, "If he couldn't do his music, he would be lost."

Kanye West

50 Cent was not an entertainer and an avid businessman, but he was also someone who knew how to do PR and capitalize on controversies.

One of the incidents where he exhibited the knack for turning controversies to his advantage was when in 2007, while promoting his third album '*Curtis*', he made an unprecedented move.

He announced publicly that if Kanye West sold more albums than his album (both albums were due to be released on the same date), he was going to quit music, and the fans bought into the challenge, thereby helping the both of them make good sales off their album.

When 50 Cent was asked in an interview about the results of the challenge and how he felt about Kanye emerging the winner, 'Kanye west gets the trophy, 50 gets the checks'.

Check it out here:

http://jjvance.com/50cent

Printed in the USA
CPSIA information can be obtained
at www.ICGtesting.com
LVHW021550211223
766988LV00097B/5656